....WHAT'S AT ISSUE?

RICH OR POOR

Jeremy Wallis

www.heinemann.co.uk/library
Visit our website to find out more information about **Heinemann Library** books.

To order:
- Phone 44 (0) 1865 888066
- Send a fax to 44 (0) 1865 314091
- Visit the Heinemann Bookshop at www.heinemann.co.uk/library to browse our catalogue and order online.

First published in Great Britain by Heinemann Library, Halley Court, Jordan Hill, Oxford OX2 8EJ, a division of Reed Educational and Professional Publishing Ltd. Heinemann is a registered trademark of Reed Educational & Professional Publishing Limited.

OXFORD   MELBOURNE   AUCKLAND   JOHANNESBURG   BLANTYRE
GABORONE   IBADAN   PORTSMOUTH NH (USA)   CHICAGO

© Reed Educational and Professional Publishing Ltd 2002
The moral right of the proprietor has been asserted.

All rights reserved. No part of this publication may be reproduced, stored in a retrieval system, or transmitted in any form or by any means, electronic, mechanical, photocopying, recording, or otherwise without either the prior written permission of the Publishers or a licence permitting restricted copying in the United Kingdom issued by the Copyright Licensing Agency Ltd, 90 Tottenham Court Road, London W1P 0LP.

Designed by Tinstar Design (www.tinstar.co.uk)
Illustrations by Nicholas Beresford-Davies
Originated by Ambassador Litho Ltd
Printed in Hong Kong/China

ISBN 0 431 03556 3   (hardback)   ISBN 0 431 03564 4   (paperback)
06 05 04 03 02   06 05 04 03 02
10 9 8 7 6 5 4 3 2   10 9 8 7 6 5 4 3 2 1

British Library Cataloguing in Publication Data
Wallis, Jeremy
    Rich or poor. – (What's at issue?)
    1. Wealth – Juvenile literature 2. Poverty – Juvenile literature
    3. Wealth – Regional disparities – Juvenile literature
    I. Title
    306.3

Acknowledgements
The Publishers would like to thank the following for permission to reproduce photographs:
AKG: p6; Corbis: p28, Hulton-Deutsch p4, Bettmann pp7, 39, 40, Howard Davies p11, Jennie Woodcock p14, Jon Spaull p15, Penny Tweedie p16, Kevin Fleming pp18, 27, Dave G Houser p24, Daniel Laine p25, Brian Harding p32, Jonathan Blair p34, Dean Conger p41, AFP p42; Cumulus: Steve Benbow: p30, Library of Congress p36, pp37, 38; John Birdsall: pp12, 26; Rex Features: p31, Sipa Press p8, 21, David Browne p10; Stone:John Millar: p22.

Cover photograph: Report Digital.

Our thanks to Julie Turner (Head of Student Services and SENCO, Banbury School, Oxfordshire) for her comments in the preparation of this book.

Every effort has been made to contact copyright holders of any material reproduced in this book. Any omissions will be rectified in subsequent printings if notice is given to the Publisher.

Any words appearing in the text in bold, **like this**, are explained in the Glossary.

Contents

Rich or poor – a modern argument? 4
Wealth and social class 6
A world of rich and poor 8
Inequality, poverty and migration 10
Health and inequality 12
Personal health and poverty 14
Poverty, health and indigenous people 16
Malnutrition and illness 18
Poverty and the HIV/AIDS epidemic 20
Housing in Britain 22
Housing in the developing world 24
The 'underclass' 26
The Bell Curve. Do our genes make us rich? 28
Education and opportunity 30
Higher education 32
Education in developing countries 34
The Great Depression 36
After the Depression 38
What causes poverty? 40
The future? 42
Glossary 44
Contacts and helplines 46
Further reading 47
Index 48

Introduction

'One for you, one for me...'

As children, we are encouraged to share and share alike, something we learn with brothers, sisters, or our friends in the playground. But in the modern world wealth, possessions and **resources** are not shared equally. Many things – access to education, career opportunities, health care – are dependent on wealth.

How have extremes of wealth and poverty developed? Why is it that, as nations have grown richer, the way money is shared within them actually becomes more unequal? Why have some nations got poorer, and others richer? Are we as individuals at fault for our own circumstances or are they caused by factors beyond our control? This book examines some of the arguments and facts to help you make up your own mind.

Rich or poor – a modern argument?

There are many questions about how wealth is divided, and many complicated arguments surround the issue. Some have been going on for thousands of years! In Ancient Greece, an Athenian ruler called Solon introduced a **democratic** system to balance the rich and the poor. Years later, the philosopher Plato said this was still the main cause of conflict in Athens.

'Democracy,' argued one Greek aristocrat, 'is a device for exploiting the rich and putting money into the pockets of the poor.' Inequality was a theme often used by the Greek dramatists.

A divided history: schoolboys outside gates of Lord's cricket ground during the Eton v Harrow match, 1937.

Two arguments

By the end of the 5th century BC, political thought had taken two main directions. One saw both nature and human beings as social and cooperative. The second said people were instinctively selfish and only interested in themselves.

The debate about how **resources** should be divided has been going on ever since. At its root is an argument about who we are as social beings and how we behave towards others. Today, some people argue for a more equal distribution of wealth because they believe it is morally wrong to allow a few to control too much wealth. They also argue that it is in everyone's interest to share the world's resources more equally.

Opponents of this argument claim the accumulation of wealth is natural and desirable. They say those with **innate** abilities – for business, sport, or singing, who are more beautiful or have more interesting things to say – should benefit from them. Some also claim the poor will always be poor, because poverty is built into people's behaviour, culture and character, that it is culturally or genetically predetermined. They think we should do nothing to interfere with the way wealth is shared out.

But others ask that if poverty is culturally or genetically predetermined, why do the numbers affected by poverty change so much over short periods of time? They argue that it is changing circumstances that cause poverty, and we must consider the welfare of all and find ways to reduce the bad effects of change.

Winners and losers

Those who believe in inequality say we have no duty to anyone but our families and ourselves, even claiming there is no such thing as 'society'. People are naturally competitive, they argue. Competition frees the most creative and intelligent aspects of our personalities. To have winners there must be losers and no one should be held back.

In the 2500 years since the time of the Ancient Greeks, wealth, poverty and inequality has provoked furious, sometimes violent, argument. The way riches have been distributed has stimulated the spread of religions such as Christianity; provoked revolutions like those in France, Russia, Mexico, Germany, Cuba, China; civil wars in England, Spain, the United States; independence struggles in Latin America, Ireland, Italy, throughout Africa and Asia; strikes and undemocratic movements around the world. Watching TV, it becomes obvious how many newsworthy events – elections, riots, wars, revolutions, civil wars, and military takeovers – are linked to the distribution of wealth. Why do you think these debates about 'who gets what' become so fierce? What do you think might happen if inequality gets worse? When resources become scarce or more expensive, will they become another source of conflict? Is extreme inequality an issue we should tackle now to stop more terrible conflicts in the future and protect the welfare of future generations? What efforts have people made to reduce inequality? Or is inequality something beyond our control – like the work of a giant, invisible hand – that we cannot, in the long term, do anything about?

Wealth and social class

Grouping people by social rank, or class, is as old as society itself. Sometimes it is by religion or race – an example is the caste system in India. Social differences are shown by the caste each Indian is born into. The Brahmin or priest caste is at the top while the so-called 'untouchables' are at the bottom. Based on the idea of reincarnation (rebirth), caste membership is seen as a consequence of conduct in the previous life.

Workers and aristocracy

Grouping people according to where they fit in society has often been done according to wealth. The independent cities of Ancient Greece were divided into distinct social classes. The majority were tradesmen and artisans (skilled workers) whose lives could be very insecure. There was a small, wealthy **aristocracy**. Extremes of wealth and poverty ensured that **democratic** life in the city was fiery and sometimes violent.

Patricians and plebs

In Ancient Rome, politics was also about rich and poor – between the aristocracy (patricians) and the common people (plebeians). Many famous Roman rulers kept the favour of the people by providing 'bread and games'. Christianity found its first believers among the very poorest subjects of the Roman **Empire**.

The Roman Games were used to keep the poor majority of Roman citizens happy.

Peasants and nobles

In Medieval Europe, wealth was based on land. The feudal system meant that everyone from peasant to noble to monarch owed their living to the person above and had a debt of service to them. (The monarch, it was believed, owed his power to God.) Violent upheavals often threatened the feudal system, for instance, the Peasants' Revolt in England.

George Orwell, author of *1984* and *Animal Farm*, called England 'the most class-ridden country in the world'.

These **uprisings** were often religious, predicting a 'Heaven on Earth' where wealth was abolished and land held equally by all. They usually occurred during times of natural calamity such as the Black Death (a plague that swept through Europe and Asia in the 14th century) or periods of high unemployment, when people's fears were strongest.

Many people have tried to define what puts a person in a particular 'class'. Is it just wealth? Or a combination of things – accent, where a person lives, income, occupation? Some people think it is the difference between those who eat 'dinner and tea' and those who eat 'lunch and dinner'! While there is no generally agreed definition of social class, and some politicians argue there is 'no such thing as class' or that we are 'classless', everyone agrees that social division exists.

SOCIAL MOBILITY

In modern industrial societies, class division is less rigid. People have 'social mobility', which means they can, over generations or even their own lifetime, move up the social scale. Ask your parents or grandparents what *their* grandparents did and where they came from. It is an interesting way of charting social mobility from a personal point of view.

FACT

Every ten years the British Government carries out a census or count of the population. It classes people according to how they fit one of seven occupational groups:
I   Professional occupations
II Managerial and technical occupations
III N Skilled non-manual occupations
III M Skilled manual occupations
IV Partly-skilled occupations
V   Unskilled occupations
VI Armed forces
Because of changes in the way people work and in society, this system is being reviewed.

A world of rich and poor

To many people growing up in a **developed country**, the world is alive with possibilities. It is easy to be swept up in the excitement of new technology, the Internet and **e-commerce**. But don't forget – the world is harshly divided. Even in Britain there is a gulf between wealth and need. Only in New Zealand have income inequalities widened more than in Britain since 1980.

There are millions throughout the world for whom life is a struggle; where family and social relationships are shaped by poverty; where extremes of wealth and hardship create crime, illness and war; where life, as the English philosopher Thomas Hobbes said, is 'nasty, brutish and short'.

RICH FACTS

There are individuals so rich they can change the economic balance of nations. They can control media and governments, buy entire football teams or control sporting competitions. There are sports personalities and pop-stars better known for their wealth and lavish lifestyles than for their prowess on pitch or stage.

- According to War on Want, the richest 20 per cent of the world's people now receive over 150 times more income than the poorest 20 per cent.
- There are 358 dollar-billionaires in the world.
- The world's three richest billionaires have **assets** greater than the total economic output of the least developed countries and their 600 million people.

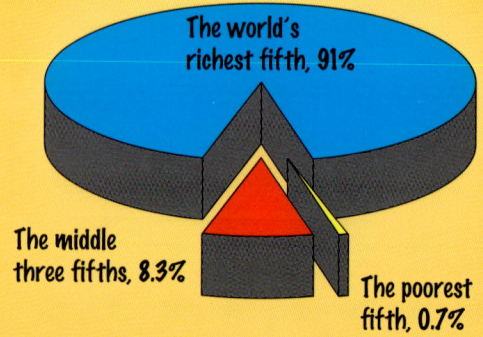

The world's richest fifth, 91%
The middle three fifths, 8.3%
The poorest fifth, 0.7%

The real distribution of wealth amongst all people. Chart from War on Want.

Conflict and poverty go hand in hand: years of war have ruined the lives of many people in South East Asia. This child soldier is a member of the rebel army of the Kampuchean Khmer Rouge.

What is poverty?

The **World Bank** defines poverty as lacking the money needed to obtain minimum levels of food, clothing and shelter. Anyone earning less than US$1 per day (60p; Aus$1.60) does not earn enough to survive. In Europe, only around 3.5 per cent of the population (1.2 billion people) live on such a sum, but numbers are far higher in the **developing world**.

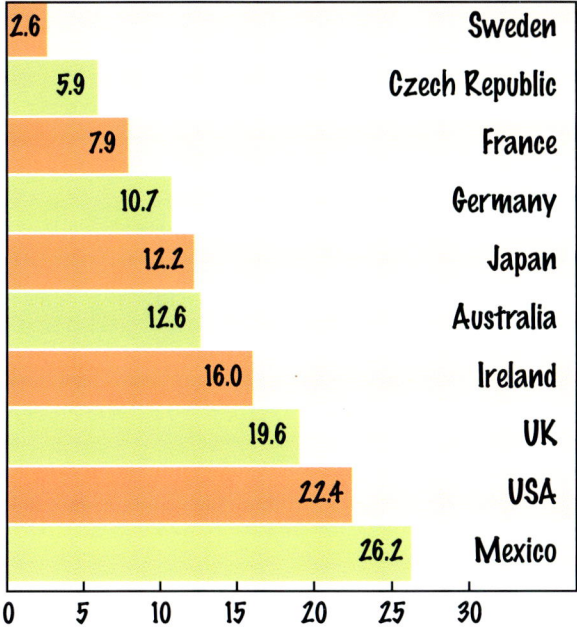

Graph from the World Bank showing per cent of children living below national poverty lines.

In rich countries, poverty is thought of in 'relative' terms – households receiving less than half of the national average income. The 'relatively poor' are excluded from the normal life enjoyed by others. Poverty re-emerged in rich countries in the 1980s, as unemployment and inequality rose.

A divided Britain

In Britain, politicians talk of 'two nations', and the 'north-south divide'. As the country grew richer, poverty increased. New wealth was concentrated in the hands of a few. Government figures in 1998 revealed one in four people (14 million) – 4.6 million of them children under 18 – lived in poverty, compared to fewer than one in ten adults and one in ten children in 1979. In 1999, Britain's top fifth of earners took 45 per cent of disposable income (the cash people have to spend). By contrast, only 6 per cent went to the poorest fifth of earners – down from 7 per cent in 1995–96, and 10 per cent in 1978.

Australia

Inequality also increased in Australia. In 1998, the poverty rate was the second highest in the developed world after the USA. Of particular concern were the numbers of homeless people and Aborigines (**indigenous** Australians) classed as poor at subsistence level (having only the bare necessities to survive).

UNICEF FACTS

In June 2000, UNICEF released figures showing the number of children living in poverty in developed nations.

UNICEF found that:
- *A child's chance of living in poverty is, on average, four times greater in single-parent families.*
- *There is a close relationship between child poverty and the percentage of households with children in which there is no adult in work.*
- *There is a close relationship between child poverty and the number of full-time workers who earn less than two-thirds of the national median wage.*
- *The countries with the lowest child poverty rates have the highest social spending.*

Inequality, poverty and migration

The greatest inequalities exist in the **developing world**, where the numbers living in poverty are staggering. According to the Catholic Fund for Overseas Development (CAFOD), of the 4.4 billion people in developing countries:
- three-fifths lack basic **sanitation**
- one-third have no access to clean water
- a quarter lack adequate housing
- a fifth have no access to health services
- a fifth of children do not finish primary school because they cannot afford to
- a fifth do not have adequate protein and energy from their food supplies.

In April 2000, **World Bank** figures showed that half the world's population survives on less than US$2 (£1.20/Aus$3.20) a day. They showed that a sixth of the earth's population – mostly in North America, Europe and Japan – receives 80 per cent of world income, an average of $70 a day.

Child labour

The International Labour Organization estimates that 120 million children aged 5–14 work full-time and a further 130 million part-time mainly in Asia, Africa and Latin America. Most children work because of poverty and raise about 20–25 per cent of family income. Some children are forced to work in the sex trade.

Poverty and migration

For hundreds of years, migrant workers – called 'swallows' – followed the harvests

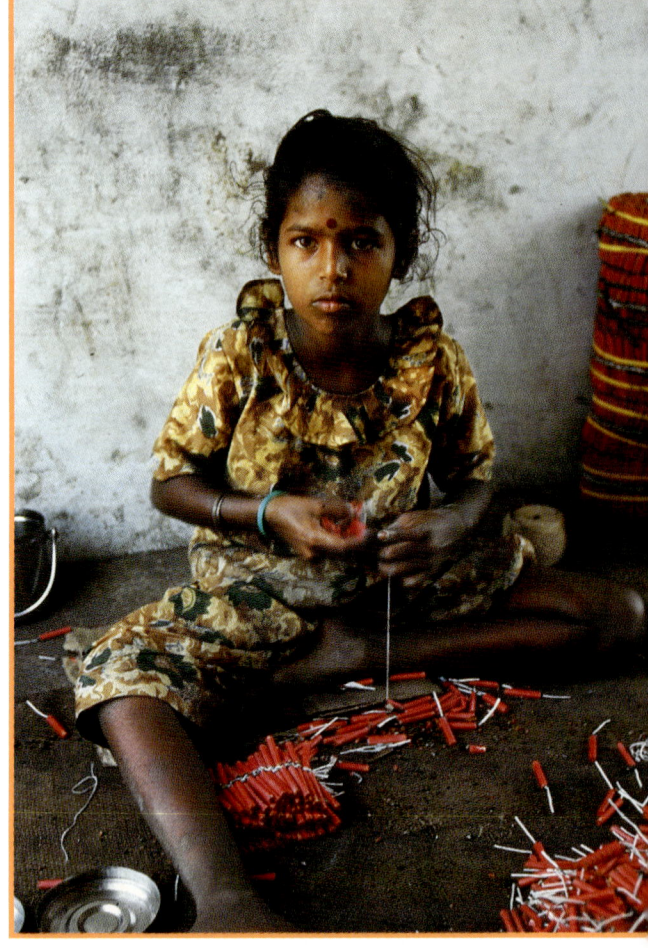

Many businesses exploit child labour in the developing world.

around Europe, like migrating birds. Today, **refugees** flee political or religious persecution and war. The last 50 years have seen an exodus of people from their homes. According to the UN High Commissioner for Refugees (UNHCR) 25 million people have been forced from their countries. Another 25 million have been internally displaced, remaining in their country but forced from their land.

> **FACT**
>
> • *Jews have always been persecuted. Ghetto is the Italian name for the area in medieval Venice where Jews had to live.*

There has been negative publicity about modern refugees and **asylum-seekers**. This is not new. In 1900, Jews were expelled from Russia and the *Daily Mail* newspaper referred to 'so-called refugees' at Southampton. 'There were Russian Jews, Polish Jews…all kinds of Jews…they hid their gold and fawned and whined and…asked for money.'

Where the grass is greener

Global images of life in countries such as Britain and the United States will always tempt migrants who want a better life for their families. In Britain, life expectancy is 77 years and **infant mortality** 6 deaths per 1000 births. It must be attractive to people from countries wracked by civil war. In Sierra Leone, for example, life expectancy is only 37 years and infant mortality is 182 deaths per 1000 births.

Poverty has spurred migration for centuries, driving the Irish to Britain, colonists to Australia and New Zealand, and migrants to America, Brazil and Argentina. Even today, Mexicans smuggle themselves across the Rio Grande to work as cheap labour in the US. But borders have now closed – the world's poor are not wanted. Mass-migration can no longer ease the pressure of poverty and population growth.

Refugees arriving at a resettlement camp. Millions of refugees around the world are condemned to live in 'temporary' refugee camps – often for many years.

Poverty and indigenous peoples

News that Christopher Columbus 'discovered' America came as a surprise to the millions already there. When settlers arrived in Australia in 1788, there were one million Aborigines. By 1933, numbers had fallen to 66,000, due to disease and conflict. Numbers now stand at 250,000. New Zealand Maoris suffered a similar fate.

> **FACT**
>
> • *In North America, the native population – 1.5 million at its height – was savagely reduced by disease and war. Lands were seized and survivors herded into special areas called reservations. After Spanish and Portuguese invaders began to arrive in South America in 1521, native numbers fell from an estimated 20 million to 1 million in just a few hundred years.*

Health and inequality

Over the last 150 years public health measures in Britain have eradicated diseases such as cholera and diphtheria. In 1900, life expectancy was 48 years for women and 44 for men; today it is 80 and 75 respectively. **Infant mortality** has plummeted from 1 in 10 to 6 in 1000.

The health gap

As early as the 19th century, **reformers** noticed higher mortality and morbidity rates amongst the poor. Even today, poor people are more likely to be ill and die younger. A child born to a poor family in Britain will live, on average, seven years less than a child born to professional parents. And it is not just years of life – the child of the poor family has a greater chance of having their life soured by long-term sickness, disability, mental illness and insecurity. The UK government calls this 'the health gap'.

- Lower occupational groups experience more illness.
- Home-owners have less illness than people who rent their homes.
- Unemployed people suffer more illness than the employed.
- There is a health gap between northern industrial areas and rich southern areas.
- The health gap is *widening*.

FACT

- *The mortality rate is the number of deaths per thousand of the population per year. The morbidity rate is the rate of illness and disease.*

For many poor people, poverty and ill-health go hand in hand.

Cancer, coronary heart disease and stroke, mental illness and accidents kill three-quarters of those who die before the age of 75.

Cancer

- Unskilled workers are twice as likely to die from cancer as professionals.
- Women in north-east England have a 33 per cent greater than average chance of developing cervical cancer.
- Rich areas have better cancer survival rates than poor.

Smoking causes a third of cancer deaths; a fifth of all cancers are of the lung. Smoking is declining, but most slowly among unskilled people. Forty per cent of unskilled men smoke, but only 12 per cent of professional men do. Diet accounts for a quarter of cancer deaths. Diets low in fruit and vegetables are linked to several cancers. Evidence suggests healthy foods can be more expensive and so an inadequate diet is normal for many families. Some bacterial infections common in poor areas are linked to stomach cancer. Several cancers are linked to industrial chemicals, affecting people who work with them or live near contaminated sites.

Coronary heart disease and stroke

Coronary heart disease (CHD) is common in the developed world. It causes damage to the heart, leading to heart attacks. Strokes are caused when an artery is blocked or ruptured, cutting off blood to the brain. CHD causes 200,000 deaths in the UK every year:

- CHD deaths in people under 65 are three times higher in Manchester than the wealthy towns of Kingston and Richmond.
- CHD kills three times more unskilled men than professionals. This gap has widened over the last 20 years.

Smoking, poor nutrition, obesity (being overweight), lack of exercise and high blood pressure increase the risk of CHD. Obesity is high among manual workers and highest among the unskilled. Some poor people's diets contain too much fat and salt, and too little fruit and vegetables. People in unskilled occupations are more likely to be less active in leisure time.

Mental health

Poor people – particularly in inner cities – are at greatest risk of mental illness, such as depression. Suicide causes 4000 deaths annually. It is three times more common in men than women, and four times more likely among unskilled men than professionals.

- Unemployed people have double the risk of depression than the employed.
- Children in poor homes have three times more mental illness than those in wealthier homes.
- Homeless people are four times more likely to have mental illness than the general population.

Risks particularly affecting poor people include poor education, unemployment, social isolation, financial problems, crime, drug/alcohol misuse, injury in the womb or at birth.

ACTION

What can you do? You could find out what is being done to improve the situation, or discover who is responsible for making changes. Is illness inevitable? Or can people help themselves become healthier? And what about you? What is your attitude to health and illness? How do you feel about your own health and well-being?
Check out these websites:
Health Education Authority – www.hea.org.uk
The Children's Society – www.the-childrens-society.org.uk
You can also search the Government's official publications website for reports on a range of poverty, health and other related topics at www.official-documents.co.uk.

Personal health and poverty

Some argue that because people *choose* to spend money on cigarettes and high-fat, high-salt foods, and *choose* not to exercise, it is their fault if they become ill.

Stubbing out cigarettes?

In 1999, the British government said, 'Smoking is the most powerful factor which determines whether people live beyond middle age.' Smoking contributes more than anything else to the 'health gap'. While many people smoke, numbers have declined, but the decline has been slowest among unskilled men and women. Why? Numbers starting to smoke are similar across social classes. But half of the better-off stop by their 30s, while three-quarters of those in the lowest income group carry on. Smoking rates are highest among people who are unemployed. They are especially high among single parents – research has shown that almost three-quarters of the poorest lone mothers smoke. One-third of all smokers in Britain are now concentrated in the poorest 10 per cent of earners. There are many reasons. Though nicotine is highly addictive and very dangerous, it can also offer short-term relief for anxiety, stress, depression, irritability, hunger – all factors particularly affecting poor people.

Many of us do not realize the harm our actions can have on others.

But do poor people simply behave in a way that harms their health more than better-off people? There are a number of things to consider:

- Even after factors like smoking have been taken into account, poor people suffer worse health than the effects of smoking and poor diet indicate.
- Advertising and the media make legal drugs such as cigarettes and alcohol very alluring.
- **Peer pressure** is a vital part of every young person's development, but it also influences decisions you must make about taking both legal and illegal drugs.
- A lot of people cannot find support to stop bad habits or break addictions.
- The opportunity to exercise is often limited by such factors as heavy traffic and pollution in urban areas, poor or expensive facilities and lack of provision for cycling or walking.

Other health factors are outside a person's control. In 1998, in Lambeth, Southwark and Lewisham in London, three of Britain's poorest boroughs, it was found that people with worse adult health were more likely to have:
- been a low birth weight baby. Babies who are small at birth because of poor nutrition in the womb risk heart disease, diabetes, stroke and high blood pressure in adult life
- suffered serious illness in childhood
- had an unskilled or semi-skilled father
- lived in a home lacking basic amenities
- had relatively poor growth in childhood
- had a poor education. People with higher educational qualifications usually have better health.

FACTS

Childhood poverty is linked to:
- *respiratory disease, diabetes, cancer, heart disease and stroke in adulthood*
- *increased disability in later life. This may be due to the increased injury risk in manual occupations*
- *an increased risk of unemployment from age 36*
- *increased risk of hospital admission and increased length of stay between the ages of 36 and 43.*

Tuberculosis

Throughout the developed world, infectious diseases associated with poverty have also made a comeback. Tuberculosis (TB) thrives in poor environments and among people already weakened by poverty or **malnutrition**. For example, the Russian chief of prisons announced that 100,000 Russian inmates have active TB.

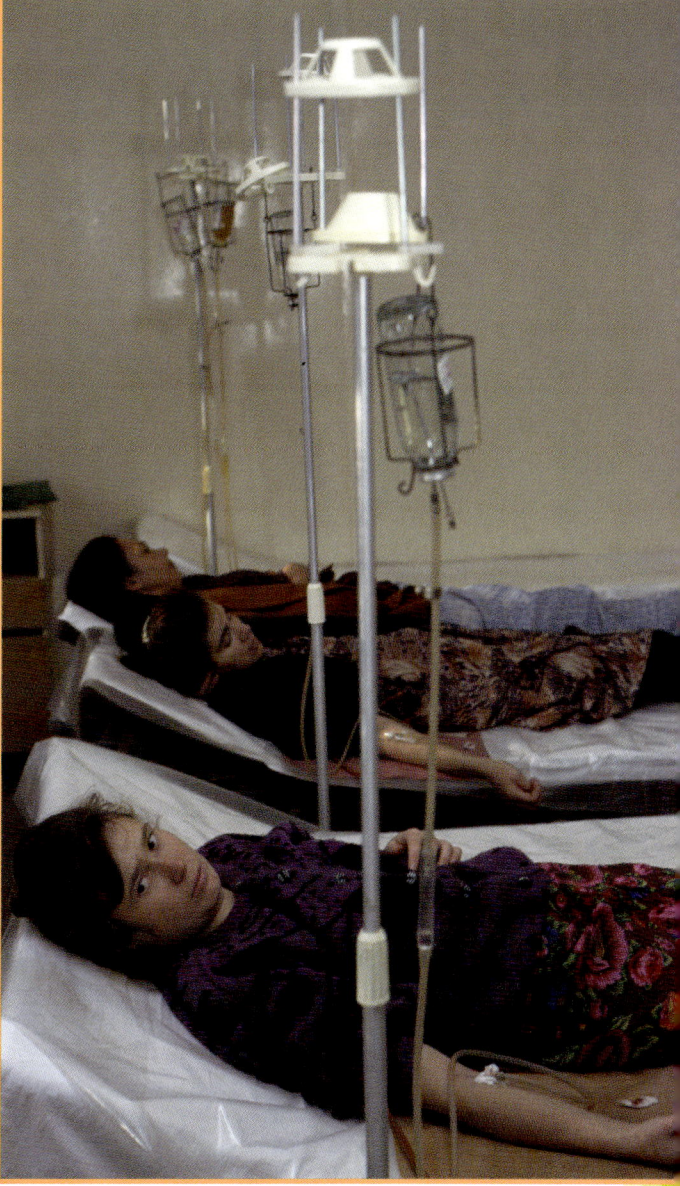

Patients being treated for Tuberculosis. Drug-resistant TB developed because many people could not afford to complete their treatment – the disease not only survived treatment but grew more powerful!

In a recent TB outbreak in the United States, several hundred people were treated in New York, one of the wealthiest cities in the world. The victims were people at the bottom of the social ladder, living in appalling conditions. Only prompt action by health workers prevented a more serious crisis.

Poverty, health and indigenous people

There are major differences in the health of the rich and poor in developed countries. This is even more striking if we look at the health of **indigenous** peoples kept out of the general increase in prosperity because of **discrimination** and **prejudice**.

By 1999, according to the Organization of Economic Cooperation and Development, the Australian **economy** had been growing continuously for nine straight years – the longest growth since the 1960s. There was employment growth, a reduction in unemployment, higher productivity – the amount produced by each person in employment – and low **inflation**. In 1999, Australian **Gross National Product (GNP)** per capita – for each person – stood at US$20,650. (Britain's stood at US$20,870.) It was a very rosy picture.

However, the Australian Bureau of Statistics reported that indigenous Australians were dying younger and in higher numbers than the rest of the Australian population. Their mortality rate was three times that of the whole Australian population. The largest differences were among people aged 35–54 years old, where death rates were 7 times higher. Fifty-three per cent of indigenous Australian men and 41 per cent of women will die before the age of 50. By contrast, in the wider Australian population, 13 per cent of males and 7 per cent of females will die before they are 50.

Many indigenous Australians have found themselves excluded from the general increase in wealth.

Links to poverty

Like most developed nations, heart disease, stroke, injury, cancer, respiratory diseases and glandular illnesses account for three-quarters of all deaths in Australia. But there were more deaths among indigenous males and females for virtually every cause:

- three times more deaths from heart disease and stroke among indigenous males; 20 times more deaths from rheumatic heart disease
- five times more deaths from respiratory diseases, and nine times more from pneumonia and influenza
- six times more deaths from glandular illnesses
- 40 per cent more deaths from cancer
- sixteen times more deaths from diabetes among females and nine times more among males.

These are all health problems that have proven links to poverty, parental poverty and **malnutrition**.

There were also many more deaths as a result of violence and accidents, drugs and alcohol – causes that have their greatest effect on poor people. For example, death rates from injury were three times greater, the death rate for murder and assault was seven to eight times higher, suicide and self-inflicted injury was 40 per cent more common among females and 70 per cent among males.

Infant mortality is also closely related to poverty. Sudden Infant Death Syndrome (SIDS) or cot death is six times more likely among indigenous males and seven times among females. Indigenous infant mortality rates are 70 per 1000 for males and 80 per 1000 for females, compared to a general Australian rate of 5 per 1000.

For many years, indigenous Australians did not benefit from the increase in wealth through the rest of Australia. The rates of premature death and ill health they now suffer are the continuing consequences of their poverty and social **exclusion**. It is not just in Australia: higher than average death rates have also been found amongst the indigenous natives of New Zealand, Brazil, Mexico and North America.

FACT

- *GNP per capita lets us compare the wealth of countries with small populations to that of more populous countries. GNP divided by the population gives the per capita – per person – wealth. To make comparisons even easier, it is shown in US dollars. If we compare Switzerland (population less than 7 million, GNP of US$286 billion in 1995) with the United States (population almost 249 million, GNP US$7100 billion), we see that in 1995, Switzerland had a GNP per capita of US$40,630, while the US only had a GNP per capita of US$26,980.*

ACTION

Want to know more? Check out the Australian Bureau of Statistics website for information on a range of social and economic topics – www.abs.gov.au. There are also many library books about the treatment of indigenous peoples.

Malnutrition and illness

Our idea of **malnutrition** is usually a child with stick-like limbs, a wrinkled sack of bones, eyes vacant in a face old before its time. Famines are dreadful, but despite the distressing image, they are unusual, normally made worse by conflict or natural disaster. However, malnutrition is usually a more gradual and subtle process – a cruel combination of poor diet and frequent illness. Poor nutrition in early life lowers resistance to disease, causes poor physical growth and interferes with brain development.

At the moment, children under five account for more than a quarter of global deaths. Almost all of these are in the **developing world**, where, according to UNICEF, malnutrition affects one-third of all under-fives. It does not have to be extreme. Of the 13 million under-fives who die every year, 7 million are malnourished. Of these, 5.6 million are only mildly or moderately malnourished. Beating malnutrition also means tackling diseases that thrive in bodies weakened by poor nutrition. Eighty-five per cent of deaths (10.6 million) are the result of infectious diseases, nearly half of them diarrhoeal diseases, such as cholera. Lives can be saved relatively cheaply – through vaccination, **oral re-hydration therapy (ORT)**, provision of clean water and basic education. However, many developing countries find themselves in difficult financial situations and unable to afford these life-saving measures.

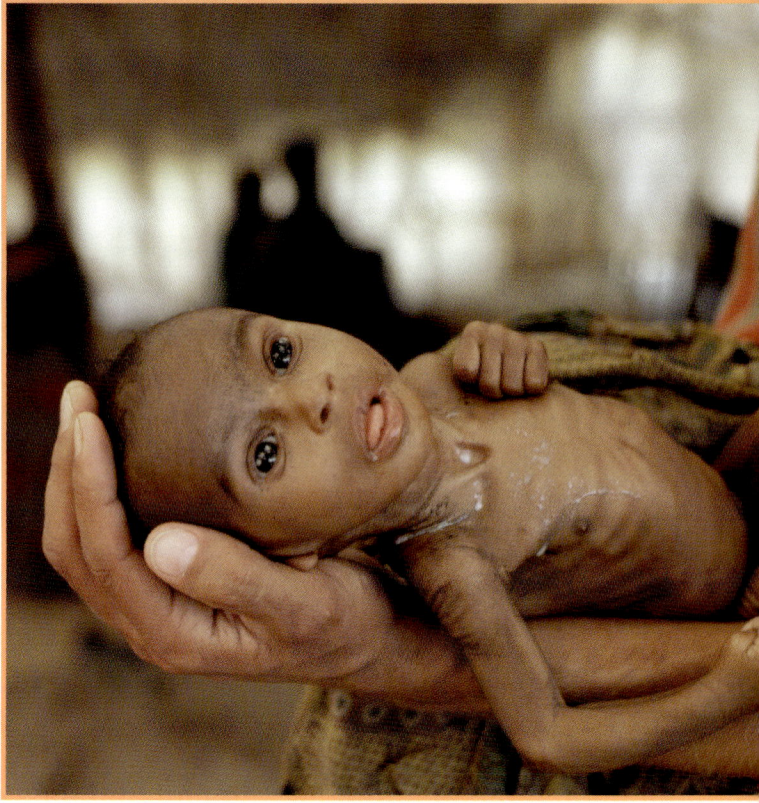

Shocking though this image might be, headline-grabbing famines actually kill far fewer people than slow malnutrition.

FACT

● *Malnutrition affects the health of the next generation even before it is born. A pregnant mother's diet has a huge impact on the child she carries. Babies weighing less than 2.5 kilograms at birth have 40 times the risk of dying soon after, and a 50 per cent greater risk of serious developmental problems, heart disease, diabetes and premature death in adulthood.*

According to UNICEF, over 20 million babies born each year – mostly in developing countries – weigh less than 2.5 kilograms. Causes include inadequate nutrition before and during pregnancy, teenage pregnancy, workload during pregnancy and smoking. Seventy per cent of underweight babies are born in South Asia and sub-Saharan Africa. Improving the nutrition of adolescent girls and pregnant women can go a long way in preventing this problem.

The effects of war

Major famines occurred in Ethiopia in the 1980s and in 2000, during times of war. The causes were environmental – no rain fell, crops failed, cattle died – but conflict made it more difficult for Ethiopia to help its own people. In Somalia in the 1990s, the government collapsed and the country split into rival chiefdoms. International relief agencies withdrew, disease ran wild and ordinary people starved. War also creates huge **refugee** crises that increase the risk of famine, malnutrition and disease.

Disease

Many serious, often fatal, diseases are preventable. For example, cholera is a water-borne infection that causes violent diarrhoea and can kill within 24 hours. Treatment normally involves re-hydrating the patient and replacing lost minerals. Cholera killed thousands in the cities of Victorian Britain but was eradicated by **sanitation** and other public health measures. Cholera recently returned to Latin America in **epidemic** proportions – in October 1993, 900,000 cases were detected and 8000 people died. Soon after, a new strain (type) emerged in southern Asia causing a second epidemic. Diseases such as cholera, pneumonia, influenza ('flu'), TB and measles have the greatest impact on people already weakened by poverty and malnutrition.

WHAT IS TO BE DONE?

Death rates from many diseases have fallen in the developing world, thanks to simple hygiene measures and education. However, many of the causes of disease are beyond the control of ordinary people. These include flood, drought and famine, war, economic change, population growth, migration, inadequate health provision and changes to ecosystems. There are also problems linked to the lack of trained personnel such as doctors, scientists and public health officials.

The issue is not how individuals can protect themselves but what large organizations – especially governments – can do. And whether they can afford to do anything at all. Developing countries lack **resources**, skills and money. Also, as you will see, the **HIV/AIDS** epidemic and debt repayment are now placing huge and growing burdens on the social structure and **economies** of many developing countries.

ACTION

To find out more about disease and malnutrition in the developing world, visit these websites:
UNICEF – www.unicef.org
World Health Organization – www.who.int
Cafod – www.cafod.org.uk
Discovery Online – www.discovery.com

Poverty and the HIV/AIDS epidemic

Every minute, six young people are infected with the **AIDS** virus. Some 2.3 million people died of AIDS in 1997, and it is among the top ten killers worldwide. Africa suffers the most. Of 13 million AIDS deaths worldwide, 11 million have been in sub-Saharan Africa. 23 million Africans are infected – two-thirds of all cases. In Botswana, Namibia, Swaziland and Zimbabwe HIV is present in 20–26 per cent of 15-49-year-olds. In some parts, life expectancy has fallen by ten years.

Cause, consequence, cure

The **epidemic** has been caused by a lethal combination of factors – sexual behaviour, other sexually transmitted diseases, which leave people open to HIV infection, poverty, **malnutrition** and poor diet, mother to baby transmission at birth, the high cost of treatment. According to the Joint United Nations Programme on HIV/AIDS (UNAIDS), health systems across Africa are devastated:

- nurses and doctors fall ill and die from AIDS
- HIV-infected patients occupy 50–80 per cent of hospital beds
- one year of basic medical costs for an AIDS patient is equivalent to two to three times a country's average yearly **GDP** per person.

Studies show that when AIDS strikes, agricultural production falls, threatening food supplies in town and country. The epidemic threatens to wipe out all the gains the **economy** has made in the last fifty years.

This map shows the impact of the AIDS/HIV epidemic throughout the world.

New drugs have cut death rates in the US and Western Europe. In May 2000, drugs companies announced a cut in treatment costs for developing nations, from US$16 dollars a day to US$2. However, 89 per cent of people with HIV/AIDS live in developing countries that account for less than 10 per cent of global **GNP**. With most of the population living on less than $2 a day, treatment is still expensive.

Effects on children

Because AIDS kills young adults, it leaves orphans. By 1998, a total of 8.2 million children had lost one or both parents to AIDS. For some of Africa's child soldiers, the **militias** are the only family they have known. While close relatives take some children in, urban growth, social disorder and migration are destroying family structures.

Prejudice and disgrace are still attached to AIDS. Because of these, many sick people do not visit clinics. In 1999, a South African AIDS campaigner, Gugu Dlamini, was beaten to death by a gang after announcing she was HIV-positive. 'Her death reminds us how stigmatizing AIDS still is, and how much courage it takes for people with HIV to be open about their condition,' UNAIDS Director, Peter Piot, said.

The developed world

HIV/AIDS is still a major problem in the developed world. Once ignorantly dismissed as a gay plague, it has rapidly become an illness of the poor. In the US, AIDS is the leading killer of young black men and the second leading killer of young black women. Prevention efforts in the US have not yet paid off – 75,000 people became infected in 1998, as many as the year before.

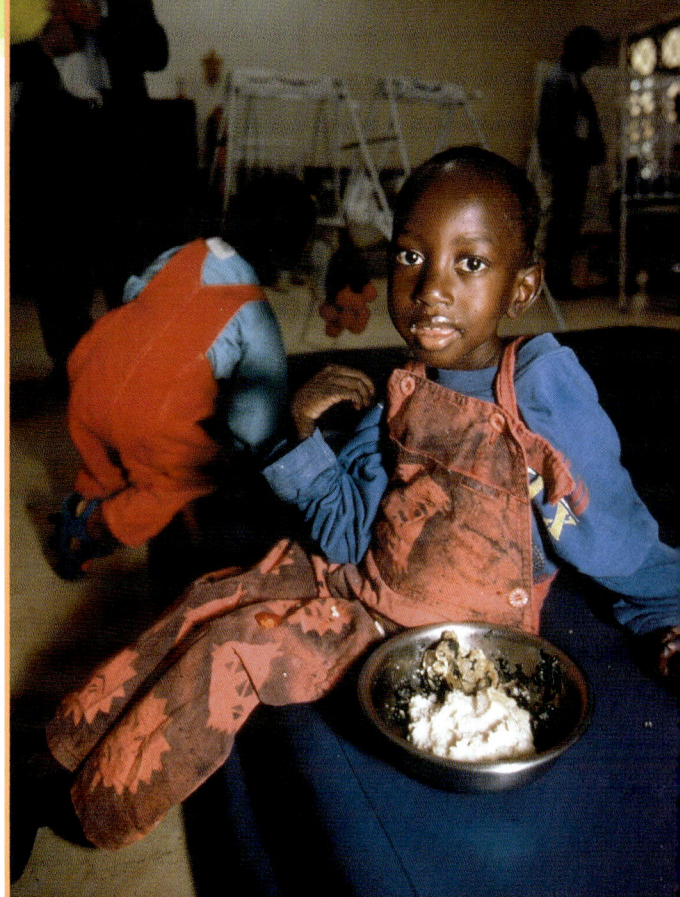

Children in an AIDS orphanage. Malnutrition and disease normally affects the young and the old: AIDS is wiping out the middle generation, leaving the elderly and the young to fend for themselves.

FACT

- In Uganda, an education drive has encouraged Ugandans to delay the age of first sexual experience, take fewer partners and use condoms. New infections have dropped from 239,000 in 1987 to 57,000 in 1997. A workable HIV vaccine will also save lives. In 2000, the British Medical Research Council announced the start of human trials of a vaccine. Developments in understanding mother-to-child transmission also promise to reduce child infections where pregnant women can be tested.

Housing in Britain

After food, shelter is crucial to survival. Britain's cities grew because industry needed workers and because **enclosure** of land drove people from the countryside. City life had rewards, but dirty and overcrowded conditions meant the poor fell victim to such diseases as cholera, typhoid, polio and diphtheria. For years, people campaigned to have neighbourhoods rebuilt.

Streets in the sky

As the first industrial nation, Britain was like a huge laboratory of everything that could go right and wrong during urbanization. The government soon realized that everyone benefited from proper sanitation and housing. By the middle of the 20th century, slums were replaced by tower blocks – 'streets in the sky'. But as old problems were solved, new ones emerged.

JACK THE RIPPER – HOUSING REFORMER?

Nineteenth-century Whitechapel, in London's East End, was a festering warren of slums. Demands for change were ignored. Finally, the outcry following Jack the Ripper's 'ghastly 'orrible murders' provoked action. The area was transformed with model dwellings, workshops, lighting and new **sanitation**.

Newer housing schemes have created as many problems as they solved.

Renting and buying

In 1979 in Britain, 32 per cent of all housing was rented from local councils. By 1996, it was only 18 per cent. The number of people living in their own homes rose from 55 to 67 per cent. The 1980s Right To Buy (RTB) policy encouraged people renting council houses to buy them. According to the organization Shelter, 216,130 council houses were sold under RTB in London alone. But local councils were prevented by central government from replacing houses. In north-east England, 2970 houses were sold, but only 10 were built. RTB left many local councils with the houses in which no one wanted to live.

In many areas today, especially London and the south-east, high house prices leave many people, even those in work and on good wages, unable to buy a home. Meanwhile, in poorer regions where there is little work, house prices are standing still or falling, so home-owners cannot afford to move to areas with jobs. In Britain as a whole, 14 per cent of all households live in poor housing – houses that are very damp, in disrepair or needing modernization. Poor people are most likely to live in bad housing. Most poor housing is in the large cities, and levels are twice as high in deprived areas. People in poor areas, living in poor housing, also suffer from social **exclusion**. The Government set up a Social Exclusion Unit (SEU) to tackle the problems they face.

In the country

Housing problems are not confined to the city. Wealthier people move to the country to find a better environment. They often commute to the city, adding to pollution and making the urban environment worse. Many people have a second home or a holiday cottage in the country. The process spoils the countryside. Villages are empty during the week, businesses decline, local people are unable to buy homes and, like poor people through the ages and throughout the world, they move to towns and cities to find accommodation.

> ### FACT
>
> *Social exclusion describes what happens in areas with high unemployment, poor skills, low incomes, run-down housing, high crime rates, poor health and family breakdown. The Social Exclusion Unit (SEU) revealed that in Britain:*
> - *40 per cent of crime happens in only 10 per cent of the total area*
> - *10 per cent of residents are burgled once or more a year, every year*
> - *13 per cent of black people have been burgled – twice the figure for whites*
> - *racial harassment and violence is widespread*
> - *poor neighbourhoods face problems of anti-social behaviour caused by alcohol and drug abuse.*
>
> *In the 100 poorest areas, people are six times more likely to be unemployed. There is a shortage of skills and education. Robbery and attacks on staff force shops to close. Competition with supermarkets also forces small businesses to close. High crime pushes insurance beyond people's means, so they live without. Many fall prey to 'loan-sharks' who lend money at high rates of interest. Public facilities, such as schools and libraries, face bills for vandalism. This is money that would be better spent on new facilities and housing.*

Housing in the developing world

In Britain, rich and poor often share streets and villages. In some countries, however, the rich are separated from the poor. In the USA, there are communities of African-Americans, Jewish-Americans, Cuban-Americans. Even among the rich the ghetto thrives, barricaded in walled estates against the outside world.

All round the globe, rich **elites** protect themselves from urban crime with barbed wire and security guards. In South Africa, architects design towns inside high-security compounds, with houses, shops, churches, leisure centres and even jogging trails. In Brazilian cities, walled highways link rich areas with the business centres. Many cut straight through poor **shantytowns** – the *favelas*.

Brazil

Brazil has one of the most unequal **economies** in the West. Ten per cent of the population take forty-seven per cent of the income, the poorest ten per cent earn less than one per cent. Education and other services are not government priorities. Less than one in five children of the poor completes primary school. According to the World Health Organization (WHO), life expectancy in Brazil is 63 years for men and 71 for women. UNICEF figures show **infant mortality** at 36 per 1000. Every year, 140,000 children die before their fifth birthday.

The favelas of Brazil. In their efforts to avoid travelling through them, many rich Brazilians now use helicopters – causing congestion in the skies above!

In Rio de Janeiro and São Paulo, the *favelas* sprawl across the hillsides, strongholds of drug gangs and poverty. In Rio they house one in five of the city's population. Visitors to São Paulo, the country's largest city, first notice luxury apartments, malls and skyscrapers.

Soweto was one of the 'townships' created by the apartheid government to keep black people and white people apart.

But built in the shadows of the buildings are shantytowns of cardboard, cinder block and corrugated tin. For most young people the choice is to join the gangs and risk an early grave or to suffer a lifetime of unemployment or menial labour. For a few, like the football player Romario, there is another way out.

In nations like Brazil, three or four generations might share accommodation in the *favela*. While a fortunate few might work in relatively well-paid jobs in factories owned by companies like Ford and Volkswagen, wages are still too low to support the whole family. Everyone who can must work. Child-care is entrusted to grandparents or great-grandparents.

South Africa

Johannesburg is the largest city in South Africa. It was founded after the discovery of gold in the Witswatersrand and is a centre of diamond processing, gold and commerce. Crime is a major problem with 300 street robberies a day. Rates of murder and assault are high. The city is ringed with shantytowns and townships built by the **apartheid** government for the black people who worked in the city. The most famous is Soweto (*South-West Township*). It was the scene of a major **uprising** against apartheid in 1976. Today it is still wracked by poverty and crime. **AIDS** fills Soweto's orphanages with sick, abandoned children.

Many settlements lack electricity, **sanitation**, education and health care. In Alexandria Township, six or more people sleep in cramped rooms of houses

constructed from cinder blocks, old doors, tarpaulin, packing cases, even crushed coke cans. Like in Victorian England, extremes of wealth and poverty can be found next to each other in South Africa. You can see an executive barking into his mobile phone alongside a street-hawker selling statues made from wire; businessmen waiting for taxis where migrant workers sell single cigarettes.

Though ended, apartheid marked South Africa in many ways. Most whites live in secure suburbs, most blacks in townships. Most whites are rich, most blacks poor. However, South Africa still has as many as four million illegal immigrants. For many people, the search for a better life stumbled to a halt in the squatter camps. Not good, but better, perhaps, than Mozambique, Angola, Congo or Rwanda. South Africa has a male life expectancy of only 52 and a **GNP** per person of US$3210. But it compares well to Rwanda, for example, where male life expectancy is less than 40 and GNP per person is US$210.

25

The 'underclass'

In the 1990s, politicians and social scientists began to talk about an 'underclass' that was missing out on the general increase in prosperity. A vocabulary developed to describe them – 'long-term unemployed', 'chronically unemployable', and the ominous 'underwolves' that conjured up a picture of disorderly criminal predators. Different people were blamed for 'creating' the underclass – single parents, teenage mothers, absent fathers, fraudsters, teachers, minorities. Welfare benefits and the 1960s' sexual revolution were also blamed. Charles Murray, an American **sociologist**, claimed Britain was following the USA, where state welfare payments have created a dependency culture – a cycle of unemployment (and aversion to work), crime and single motherhood. 'A plague is spreading through our social fabric', he stated. In fact, single parenthood is usually caused by divorce. According to sociologist Joan Brown, the idea of marriage has been challenged throughout the whole of society.

Some people believe we have created an underclass on the run-down estates of our major cities.

The Thatcher era

Some people said the underclass was not new but consisted of people who had not adapted to the changes in the **economy** that took place in the 1980s. The election of Margaret Thatcher's Conservative government in Britain, in 1979, marked the beginning of major changes in the way governments managed their economies. The governments of developed countries abandoned their aim of employment for everyone and the idea that the countries needed heavy industry, manufacturing or mining to be strong. Such work could be left to nations with cheap labour, such as South Korea, Mexico, Taiwan and China. Instead, employment would be left to market forces.

MARKET FORCES

In the 1980s it became popular to claim that everything was the consequence of market forces. The idea is that the relationship between people buying and people selling decides everything in an economy – the type of products, the price and the quantity. The inefficient producer who makes things too expensive, or the wrong colour or style will either change or go bust. Meanwhile, the producer who gets it right does well. For market forces to work properly, government meddling, or regulation, had to be kept to a minimum.

Throughout the 1980s and 1990s, governments followed policies of **deregulation** based on this political and economic idea of market forces, leading to a free market. People who believe in free markets argue that employment levels, wages, distribution of wealth, working conditions, profits, prices, **inflation**, education, health, even fashion and pop music benefit from the free operation of the market.

Cycle of deprivation

For years, Britain enjoyed full employment, the unemployed being mostly people between jobs. After 1979, however, large labour-intensive industries were allowed to close. Labour-intensive refers to industries that rely on many workers, such as factories and mines. This left many areas without work. Unemployment rose sharply, beginning a cycle of deprivation – the end of full employment caused unskilled workers to fall off the bottom of the occupational ladder and become the underclass.

Major industries – coal-mining, steel, car-making, textiles, shipbuilding – declined or disappeared. Most of Britain's poorest areas are concentrated where these industries once were: the north-east and north-west of England; Scotland; Wales; the West Midlands; Yorkshire; Nottinghamshire; Merseyside.

Deregulation made the division of the country's wealth more unequal, says sociologist Gary Runcimon. It created a super-rich **elite** and a low-skilled, poorly educated service class (cleaners, fast-food workers, and so on). The creation of an underclass – the long-term unemployed – in many countries was part of this re-structuring. People who were unemployed because their skills were no longer wanted in turn created a generation without any skills at all.

The end of heavy industries like ship building in the 1980s meant a huge increase in the number of unemployed people where those industries had once been located.

27

The Bell Curve. Do our genes make us rich?

In 1994, **sociologists** Charles Murray and Richard Herrnstein published a book called *The Bell Curve: Intelligence and Class Structure in American Life*. The bell curve is a bell-shaped line on a graph showing income distribution in the USA. It starts low because of the relatively few people on low earnings, rises to show the number on middle incomes, then drops to illustrate the minority earning high incomes. Because a line measuring the distribution of **IQ** in the USA fits over the income line, Murray and Herrnstein claimed it proved a link between IQ and income, that the rich are also an intellectual **elite**.

Innate differences

The Bell Curve argues that poverty and the division of society into ranks are not caused by economic factors but **innate** differences in intelligence. Intelligence decides a person's education, businesses hire smart people, educated people get the best jobs. People with a low IQ fall behind. Because low IQ causes poverty and unemployment, government policies to alleviate them actually create a dependency culture – a circle of unemployment, family breakdown, crime and reliance on state benefits. *The Bell Curve* argues that birth rates should be encouraged among intelligent families, and discouraged among those with a low IQ by ending measures to help them, such as state benefits.

The authors also claim that black people have lower IQs. Racism, they said, has little to do with inequality. When people of similar IQ are compared, blacks are

Hitler believed that the Germanic (Aryan) people were superior to any other and used eugenics to help keep the race pure.

28

more likely than whites to be doctors, lawyers, teachers and engineers. Differences in income and employment disappear, showing that inequality is due to IQ, not racism. They also argued that low-IQ immigrants threaten American society, and low-IQ migrants should be barred. Unless 'inferior people' stop having so many children, they argued, developed nations will become states where tyrannical **elites** rule urban reservations of the low-IQ underclass. Opponents of Herrnstein and Murray's ideas claim they are recommending a policy of eugenics (selective breeding).

FACT

● *At the end of the 19th century, the theory of eugenics was developed. It claimed that humankind could be improved by selective breeding. Since then, it has been used to justify policies based on class or race. Those who believed in eugenics blamed Britain's slow progress in the Boer War (1899–1902) on the 'degeneration [decline] of the Imperial Race'. Others realized that the frailty of British soldiers was a result of childhood poverty so free milk was introduced in schools. In the 1930s, Hitler used the eugenics theory to justify the* **sterilization** *and murder of disabled and mentally ill people, gypsies, Jews and the Slavs of the east. It was not just Nazi Germany. By 1943, 30 US states allowed sterilization of 'genetically unfit' individuals. Sweden had a policy of sterilization until the late 1960s. The former South African government followed a policy of 'separate development' (apartheid is Afrikaans for 'apartness').*

A flawed theory

Other social scientists have discovered that IQ scores in children have risen sharply over the past 50 years, and gaps in scores between all **ethnic** groups are closing. It has also been shown that Herrnstein and Murray chose statistics that fitted conveniently with their theories in *The Bell Curve*. IQ measurement has also been disputed since the early 20th century, because many supporters believed that intellectual development and social standing were fixed at birth.

The science is also not at all exact. In a reformatory (youth custody centre) in America, for example, every new inmate was tested from the 1930s on. In the 1940s, the average IQ jumped up, not because inmates became more intelligent, but because a different IQ test was introduced! For years in the Czech Republic, tests labelled gypsy children 'retarded'. But the tests did not accept cultural and language differences – most intelligent people would fail a test in a language they do not understand.

In the genes

However, the more we learn about **genes** and how they affect us, the more likely it seems that there *is* some genetic foundation to character, personality and intelligence. It seems equally unlikely, however, that they are solely the product of our genes. Learning from others as we grow up is a crucial part of making us who we are, and every one of us has opportunities we can make use of. As we will see, education is a very good example of these opportunities.

29

Education and opportunity

Even including winning the National Lottery, education is your best means of getting on in life! For every millionaire who dropped out of school, there are thousands who did not, and thousands of drop-outs who are not millionaires. The Institute of Education in London found academic achievement the single most important factor in later success. In the **developing world**, meanwhile, both **HIV/AIDS** and basic health care prove that education can mean the difference between life and death.

Whether a person can benefit from education or not often depends on wealth. In Britain, people from low-income households must overcome significant hurdles. In *A Class Act*, Andrew Adonis and Stephen Pollard describe Britain's school structure as 'educational **apartheid**' – the separation of social classes and systems. Wealthy people have a head start the world over, but separation is greater and starts sooner in Britain.

Private schools

Seven per cent of British children – ten per cent in London – are privately educated. They pay average annual fees of £6150 for day pupils and £10,500 for boarders. A *Financial Times* survey in 1999 revealed that 87 of the top 100 schools were in the private sector. Private schools are exam hothouses employing highly qualified teachers. Private schools boast facilities better than most universities. Teachers are better paid and parents and pupils deeply committed. The average pupil/teacher ratio is 1:10, compared to the state school average of 1:18. Almost 90 per cent of private school pupils go into further education and form 25 per

Many private schools boast facilities better than many universities!

CASE STUDY

In 2000, *The Guardian* newspaper compared Stanley Deason Comprehensive School on the poverty-stricken Whitehawk estate, Brighton, with the private Roedean Girls' School. The two schools are separated only by Roedean's grassy playing fields. Roedean's results are the best in the county. Before Stanley Deason was closed in 2000, only 10 per cent of its pupils gained five or more GCSE A–C grades. Many children had fallen behind by the time they got to the school – only one in ten year seven pupils had a reading age of eleven.

cent of university entrants. But private school pupils are not **innately** more intelligent, as studies have shown.

The picture is the same in primary schools. Private pupils are four years ahead of what is expected by age eleven. By contrast, in 1996, four out of five eleven-year-olds in one London borough failed a basic reading test. State schools consistently do less well than private ones. Eighty per cent of private school pupils pass five or more GCSEs at grade A–C. In state schools, only 43 per cent reach the same standard.

Truancy and failure

In deprived areas, pupils do much worse than average. Less than 15 per cent of pupils achieve five or more GCSEs at grade A–C. On poor estates, one in four children gains no GCSEs, and truancy is four times the average.

The National Child Development Survey showed a relationship between parents' earnings and children's performance. This is important because, as the Government confirms, deprivation has trebled since

Hackney Downs School in east London was closed by the government who believed it was failing to provide adequate teaching and motivation for its pupils.

1979 and a third of Britain's children – over four million – live in poverty. The British pupil failure rate is one of the highest in the **developed world**, but child poverty is also greater.

Differences in early development must also be considered. US research shows that educational prospects can be damaged before a child is three years old if they are not 'school ready'. Key factors affecting this include birth weight, early language development, mental well-being and reading by parents. At 22 months, children of parents in higher social classes have a 14 per cent higher educational development than those in the lowest.

Higher education

The majority of pupils entering Britain's best universities – especially Oxford and Cambridge (Oxbridge) – are from private schools. Entry is difficult but because it reflects well on schools, most admit coaching pupils applying to Oxbridge.

Governments have tried to open the system. By the 1960s, state school pupils made up 62 per cent of Oxbridge students, private school pupils 38 per cent. But by the 1990s, private school numbers had risen again to over 50 per cent.

Social bias

There is also bias towards higher social classes. In 1997–8, 80 per cent of Oxbridge first-year students came from

Many people believe that Britain's best-known higher educational institutions exclude many suitable candidates because of their social background.

the highest social classes while only eight per cent of all Oxbridge students were from the three lowest. In 2000, *The Times* reported that the chances of working-class children getting into a top university were less than one in a hundred and that half those admitted to Imperial College, the London School of Economics and University College, London, were privately educated.

This bias would not be so important if it were not for the influence of Oxbridge.

OXBRIDGE CONNECTIONS

- Richard Curtis, writer of 'Blackadder', 'Four Weddings and a Funeral', 'Notting Hill' and 'Bean': Harrow School, then Cambridge, where he met actors Rowan Atkinson and Stephen Fry.
- The stars of 'Monty Python's Flying Circus' met at Cambridge and Oxford
- Nick Hancock, comedian: Cambridge
- Tony Blair, Michael Heseltine and Margaret Thatcher, politicians: Oxford
- Anselm Audley, seventeen-year-old novelist paid £50,000 for his first book: Millfield School, then Oxford
- Richard Whitely and Carol Vorderman of 'Countdown': Oxford and Cambridge respectively

Of 250 people randomly selected from the 1996 *Who's Who*, Adonis and Pollard found 114 went to Oxbridge. Of the last nineteen Prime Ministers, Oxford provided nine and Cambridge three. Oxbridge graduates dominate the BBC's News Trainee scheme. 'In every walk of…life,' they conclude, 'Oxbridge dominates. A country of 57 million people is governed by 2 per cent of her graduate total.'

A divided system

Upper-class applicants are more likely to get into prestigious universities. Half the private school applicants with three A grades at A-level were accepted at Oxbridge, compared to under a third of state school applicants with the same grades. At the LSE, King's and University College applicants from 'posh' backgrounds are more successful, compared to students from poorer households.

Figures from the Higher Education Statistics Agency reveal a divided system. Oxbridge, Bristol, Edinburgh, Nottingham, St Andrews, Durham and Imperial College, London, take 70 per cent of their students from the highest social classes. In contrast, students from these backgrounds make up only 35 per cent at the New Universities – many former polytechnics – of Central Lancashire, Thames Valley, East London, Wolverhampton and Paisley.

Changes to student finance also hit poor families – student loans mean large debts. As a consequence, many decline to enter further education. For years, many people from poorer households entered higher education as mature students. However, in April 1999, the number dropped significantly. In one year, numbers fell by 7.6 per cent in the 21–24 age group, and 10.7 per cent for over–25s.

Though degree qualifications are supposed to be 'equal', degrees from the New Universities are not always as well regarded. For example, in the legal profession, statistics show Oxbridge graduates are six times more likely to get pupillage – traineeship with a law firm after completing a degree – than graduates from the New Universities. It is not because they are brighter. An Oxbridge graduate with a lower second class degree has a better chance of getting pupillage than a New University graduate with a first class degree. Medical schools have also been singled out for not taking students from poorer backgrounds.

Education in developing countries

Many people argue that education is neither luxury nor privilege, but a basic right. Of the world's poorest children 125 million are denied basic education. This number is equal to all children between six and fourteen in Europe and North America. **Illiteracy** keeps poor countries poor. In the **developing world**:

- one in four adults is illiterate
- women are 60 per cent more likely to be illiterate
- 150 million children who start school drop out
- in the 47 least developed countries, half the children do not go to school
- sixteen African countries saw school attendance drop in the 1990s
- in the 1980s, education spending fell by 65 per cent in Africa and 40 per cent in Latin America
- in parts of Egypt there are 12 girls to every 100 boys in school
- girls throughout the world fall behind, despite proven links between girls' education and the future health of families.

People without education are extremely poor, usually unhealthy, and die decades earlier than people with an education. They are open to terrible exploitation. For example, in Sierra Leone, Angola, Burma, Cambodia and many other countries, thousands of child soldiers are mentally or physically scarred. They are taking part in wars without reason, without end, without hope. In Asia, millions of girls become family skivvies or are sold as sex slaves.

Even where there are education opportunities for poorer children in the developing world, facilities are often meagre and classes overcrowded.

Vicious cycle

Without education, a vicious cycle of ignorance, poverty and civil strife undermines nations. **Economies** crumble, countries collapse into chaos, **refugee** numbers increase. Estimates put the cost of primary education for all the world's children at US$8 billion annually. This is what the world spends on arms every four days and half what the USA spends on toys every year!

Education for all

Fifty years ago, the United Nations Declaration of Human Rights recognized education as a basic human right. In 1990, the world community promised primary education for all by 2000. In 1995, it was put back to 2015. Organizations have lobbied to make 2015 a real goal. Oxfam proposed a Global Plan of Action. In this, rich countries would provide US$4 billion a year through aid and debt relief, matched by developing countries diverting military and wasteful spending to education. Pakistan, for instance, spends six times more on the military than on primary education, while 11 million children are out of school and two in three adults are illiterate.

Many also believe the **World Bank** and **International Monetary Fund (IMF)** should change policies that demand the poor pay for education. Many cannot afford it and school enrolment rates have dropped in several countries as a result. Many governments, from Brazil to the Philippines, direct spending towards higher education that benefits the wealthy rather than towards basic education that benefits the poor.

LIFE IN SILICON–FAVELA!

In the 1990s, a computer expert opened up a computer school to teach new skills to the people of Brazil's *favelas* (shantytowns). By 2000, the Committee to Democratize Information Technology (CDI) had established 107 schools in *favelas* in 13 Brazilian states. In an interview, Rodrigo Baggio, nicknamed 'the Bill Gates of the Slums', said 'poor people in Brazil don't die of hunger, but because of a lack of opportunities'.

Schools run three-month courses to make young people computer-literate and give them useful skills. Teachers, from the *favelas* themselves, are trained by the CDI. Each earns £55 a month. The salary of nineteen-year-old Leandro, for example, makes up half his family's total income! Pupils tackle issues such as teenage pregnancy, violence and racism. They design posters and cards with social messages to teach skills and improve community awareness. 'What students want is better opportunities to earn money. That's easy. It's important to give them an understanding of social topics,' says Baggio.

The CDI has had such great success that it now works with other Latin American and African countries. Because of the respect CDI schools have in the *favelas*, no school has ever been broken into. But trouble exists outside – classrooms do not face the street to reduce risks of being hit by stray bullets! The CDI plans to put schools on the Internet, to create a digital community of *favelas*.

ACTION

Want to know more? Check out these websites:
Oxfam – www.oxfam.org.uk
United Nations Children's Fund – www.unicef.org
Christian Aid – www.christian-aid.org.uk
Save the Children Fund (UK) – www.scfuk.org.uk

The Great Depression

There have been times when poverty has been so overwhelming it has forced us to rethink all our ideas about it. The Great Depression of the 1930s was one such time. Its impact echoed around the world and it finally led to World War Two – a conflict costing almost 35 million lives. The Great Depression influenced the way governments ran their **economies** for many years after.

The Wall Street Crash

In the years after World War One, the United States became the world's most powerful nation. Between 1913 and 1929, its economy grew by 70 per cent. The New York Stock Exchange on Wall Street was the world's leading stock market. Companies raise money on a stock market by selling **shares** to **stockbrokers** and the public. These shares are then sold and bought, prices rising or falling depending on how each company is doing. Between 1927 and 1929, share prices on Wall Street rose spectacularly. This rapid rise persuaded people that prices would keep rising and that shares were a foolproof way of making money. People used their savings, borrowed from banks and even mortgaged homes to raise cash and buy more shares. Many bought shares by paying only a part of the cost, believing rising prices would allow them to pay debts and still make a profit. Many people owed huge sums. Then, on Thursday 24 October 1929, prices fell! Hoping to cash in before they lost everything, people tried to sell shares. But with everyone selling, prices fell faster and the market collapsed. Many shares were soon worthless! People owing to banks lost businesses and homes. Companies closed, throwing thousands out of work.

The effects of the Great Depression were so profound they challenged the imagination of almost every politician and policymaker around the world.

Panic!

The Wall Street Crash was not the start of the Great Depression, as it became known, but was its most dramatic episode. There had been signs for some time. Farmers had been hit by low prices and **recession** and many could not pay loans and mortgages. Banks began to cash in mortgages and confiscate farms. Many banks found themselves without cash. When customers tried to withdraw savings, banks locked their doors and refused to hand over money. This started a run on the banks – people panicked and besieged all the banks, even ones doing well. Some healthy banks were forced to close, causing even more panic!

Millions of Americans lost their jobs. Families lost homes and had to sell possessions. Without welfare, people relied on soup kitchens and homeless shelters, known as 'flophouses'. Farming families were forced from their lands in the Midwest. Many were drawn to California by the false promises of work and homes there.

Around the world

Because of the US economy's influence on the rest of the world, the Wall Street Crash made economic problems around the world much worse. Countries dependent on **exports** to the USA were hardest hit.

In Mexico, **imports** and exports fell by two-thirds and unemployment rose.

In Jarrow, north-east England, unemployment stood at 67.4 per cent in 1934. Hundreds of unemployed men marched almost 300 miles to London to publicise their plight.

It was made worse by the repatriation (enforced return) of Mexican workers from the US. In Australia, the depression increased unemployment and ended immigration. Development of industry and agriculture stopped, and agricultural exports fell.

In Britain, unemployment affected 2.9 million people. Areas that relied on exports – Scotland, the north of England and Wales – were worst hit. Only areas like south-east England remained relatively well-off. The fragile German economy was hit very hard. Unemployment was over 6 million by January 1932, from a working population of 20.5 million. In increasing numbers, desperate Germans looked to Adolf Hitler and the **Nazis** on the political extreme right, or to the revolutionary **Communists** and **Socialists** on the extreme left.

After the Depression

Until the Great Depression, **economists** believed unemployment was natural. As one source of employment declined, another developed, creating new jobs. Governments followed a *laissez faire* or 'leave alone' policy and did not interfere. But the scale of the crash was so bad something had to be done.

John Maynard Keynes

During the 1920s and 1930s, a British economist called John Maynard Keynes worked out his General Theory. It would become the foundation of economic policy in many countries until the 1970s. Normally, he said, people's spending helps to keep the economy healthy. In a depression, however, the unemployed have no money and people in work hang on to money because they are worried about the future. Keynes believed a government could increase confidence, economic growth and employment by creating jobs and stimulating demand. With increased demand comes more jobs, jobs increase people's confidence, and confidence increases spending. A government could pay for this by borrowing money. As the economy improves, increasing **taxes** can be used to repay the lenders.

In 1931 Keynes said, 'Whenever you save five shillings, you put a man out of work for a day.' He also explained that it was even better to employ a man to dig a hole then fill it in than to have him unemployed – because the worker then has wages to spend!

Trade barriers

Keynes was ignored in Britain, where governments cut spending. Because Britain had an **empire**, it was able to see off the worst effects of economic depression. It created trade barriers (special taxes) around the empire and made its colonies trade within it. Unemployment was still high, and stayed

A NEW IDEA?

Keynes' ideas were revolutionary – but not all were new. Some historians believe the Egyptian pyramids were built to keep farmers busy between harvests.

In the United States, the New Deal created thousands of jobs on huge construction and reclamation projects.

high, however. In 1941, two years after the outbreak of World War Two, there were still one million people unemployed in Britain!

Contrasting results

In 1932, Franklin D. Roosevelt was elected President of the USA. His 'New Deal' promised that the federal (central) government would use Keynesian-style measures to develop the economy. Projects included dam- and road-building programmes, environmental schemes, arts, agriculture and welfare programmes and laws controlling the minimum wage.

The contrast is interesting. In Britain, **Gross Domestic Product (GDP)** grew by 26 per cent between 1932 and 1939. In the same period, the GDP of the United States grew by 41 per cent.

The end of the Keynes era

From 1945 until 1979, almost all developed countries followed Keynesian policies to maintain full employment. However, many economists believed that full employment was difficult to keep up and caused **inflation**. From 1979, countries all over the world abandoned Keynes. Tackling inflation became the priority instead of maintaining full employment. Many anti-inflation measures – such as raising interest rates and cutting government spending – increased unemployment and pushed down wages.

FACT

- In Soviet Russia, there had been socialist rule since 1917. **Socialism** promised a society where individuals were free of the poverty and inequalities of **capitalism**. This meant ownership of industries and agriculture was taken away from individuals and put into the hands of the state. Shunned by their capitalist neighbours, Soviet governments looked inwards and were able to achieve rapid development of industry and **infrastructure**. During the first 'Five Year Plan' (1928–33), industrial output more than doubled. However, this was achieved at great cost. Millions of peasants died as a result of a policy of collectivization (state take-over) of farms, which led to famines.

Margaret Thatcher's election victory in 1979 was the beginning of the end of Keynesian-style economic management throughout the developed world.

What causes poverty?

The gap between rich and poor countries is widening. In 1960, the world's wealthiest 20 per cent had 30 times the income of the poorest 20 per cent. By 1995, they had 82 times. Some African countries are poorer now than in 1960. Since 1970, income per person of average African households has fallen by 20 per cent. Many developing nations spend over one-third of revenues (annual income) on debt repayments. Basic needs – education, health, **infrastructure** – are unaffordable.

> In 1984, while Ethiopians starved, the country was exporting food to repay its debt.

DEBT REPAYMENT

When a bank lends money, it charges interest. If £1000 is borrowed at 10 per cent annual interest, it means that £1000 (the principle) plus £100 interest must be paid back. If not paid within a year, interest builds up. Governments use interest rates to control economic activity. High interest makes borrowing expensive, so people delay buying houses, investing, and so on, and the **economy** slows down. Low interest makes borrowing cheap, so the economy speeds up.

Many countries borrowed billions of dollars at low interest rates from wealthy banks and other lenders in the West. The **World Bank** encouraged borrowing. 'There is no problem of developing countries being able to service [repay] debt,' it said in 1978. Then interest rates rose, trapping debtor nations. Unable to pay principle or interest, debts increased. Some nations, such as Ethiopia, exported food while suffering famine, to repay their debt.

For developing nations doing well, debt is a 'drag anchor' slowing economic and social development. Debt is carried by everyone, including the poor who often gain no benefit. To lessen economic problems and cut foreign debt, the Brazilian government sold off infrastructure, such as electricity companies and railways, to foreign companies – US$40 billion-worth in 1999 alone. The World Bank proposed wage and **pension** cuts and longer hours. Brazil could then borrow another US$42 billion to keep its economy afloat.

Money transferred abroad, often illegally, from countries made debt worse. At the same time as cutting wages and pensions for the poor, Brazil recently paid 40 per cent interest on savings to stop rich Brazilians sending money abroad.

FACT

- *Low **GNP** per person does not condemn people to illness if **resources** are devoted to health. Cuba (GNP per person US$1170) has **infant mortality** of 7 per 1000. This is the same as the United States, with GNP per person of US$29,080 – almost 25 times that of Cuba!*

In 1999, wealthy nations promised US$100 billion (£63 billion) for debt relief. But **International Monetary Fund (IMF)** figures show only moderate relief. Mozambique, for example, paying US$98 million a year in debt repayment would see this reduced to US$73 million. Despite debt, East Asia and Latin America have made progress. But several other factors trap many African nations in a cycle of poverty and war:

- Agricultural techniques have upset the environmental balance, with devastating consequences, for example, in Mozambique.
- **Empires** – British, French, German, Belgian – created many nations. Some are small and vulnerable, others contain a mix of **ethnic** rivalries.
- Independence left weak governments. Unstable countries were caught in vicious civil wars.
- **Apartheid** held back all of southern Africa.
- **Recessions** in developed nations hit **exports**.
- Economies have been badly managed. Many countries undertook expensive projects financed by loans.
- The IMF's 'cruel to be kind' strategy made cuts in health, education and **sanitation** a condition of debt relief.

Even healthy economies find themselves in difficulty. In 1997, the IMF and World Bank praised South Korea, Malaysia, Thailand, Indonesia and the Philippines as 'developing nations doing well by every measure'. Within months, all had collapsed into recession!

Even the fast-growing, so-called 'tiger economies' of the developing world, like Singapore, have been hit by recession and economic collapse.

41

The future?

What does the future hold where divisions between rich and poor are widening? In the **developed world**, wealth has become more concentrated. What will happen if people **monopolize** skills, education and new technology? And what will be the outcome for the underclass? As wealth becomes the only measure of a person's value in society, what will happen to the lower-paid professionals in health, education and public service?

What will be the consequences for the **developing world**? Will the monopolization of information and technology exclude them too? As rich nations claim **resources** for their own use, will future conflict be about resources – who gets them and how they are used? Meanwhile, poverty-stricken people look, with desperation, for answers to their plight. Some turn to religion, crime or revolution. Others take refuge in regional or **ethnic** identities. Some countries, like Sierra Leone, disintegrate into civil war. The chilling phrase '**ethnic cleansing**' enters the language.

'Natural' catastrophes, sometimes caused by pollution, intensive farming methods or deforestation, have their greatest impact on the poor. This is the aftermath of Hurricane Mitch in Honduras.

LAND REFORM

Around the world, people call for land reform. From Brazil to Zimbabwe, landless peasants occupy farms and stake out plots for themselves. These plots allow families to feed themselves, but do not produce a surplus that could be exported to bring in vital foreign currency.

Environmental problems and climatic change are the consequences of industrial pollution, destruction of forests, the use of destructive farming methods. They in turn produce hurricanes, floods and droughts, which have their greatest impact on the poor.

Who can help?

Many organizations – religious, charitable and political – work to ease the effects of poverty, but admit in most cases they cannot match the scale of the problem. Realistically, only governments and international bodies like the **World Bank** and **IMF** can deal with debt, education and other problems.

Self-help

People do help themselves. In Brazil, the CDI brings computer education to the *favelas*. People start **cooperatives** to buy and distribute goods. On poor estates in Britain and the US, where banks have closed and loan sharks lend at huge interest rates, people create credit unions that make low-interest loans.

Losing ground

Developed nations can also become **underdeveloped**. Russia, for example, has 13 per cent of the world's oil, 36 per cent of its natural gas, huge coal and iron-ore reserves. But **Gross National Product** fell by half in ten years, industries closed, unemployment soared and the currency collapsed. Estimates put the number surviving by barter (swapping what they grow, make or find) at between a third and a half of the population – over 50 million people. In 1998, the British Medical Journal reported that average life expectancy in Russia fell by five years between 1990 and 1994.

> ### FACT
> *Sometimes poverty can provoke the poor into wrongly blaming others for their misfortune:*
> - *Across Europe discontented and **alienated** working-class youths join **neo-Nazi** movements to victimize immigrants and **refugees**.*
> - *In Russia, **anti-Semitic** groups attack Jews.*
> - *People talk of losing jobs to 'foreigners'. Dishonest politicians make use of such sentiments.*

Governments can reduce poverty. Nations around the world used the theories of John Maynard Keynes to maintain growth and employment. In Britain, in the 1940s, a civil servant called William Beveridge designed a welfare state to protect the people's health and well-being, which became the envy of the post-war world. The 'New Deal' in the US showed it was possible to act against unemployment and **depression**.

In the developing world, the priorities are health and education. Both offer the greatest chances for people to improve their lives. Even scant resources, used properly, can have a major impact.

What does the future hold if nothing is done? David Landes, in a book called *The Wealth and Poverty of Nations*, said, 'The rich countries' task, in our interest as well as theirs, is to help the poor become healthier and wealthier. If we do not, they will seek to take what they cannot make; and if they cannot earn by exporting commodities [goods], they will export people.' There are no empty territories open for migration and development. How we deal with the differences between rich and poor now will shape all our futures.

43

Glossary

alienated people who do not feel part of society and therefore feel nothing for its rules

anti-Semitic an opinion or action against Jewish people

Apartheid South African political system based on race that denied the black majority a vote and kept them out of positions of political and economic power

aristocracy nobles usually owing positions to inherited wealth or rank

asset thing owned that represents wealth, such as a house or a factory

asylum-seeker people seeking shelter from persecution

capitalism system that allows the private ownership of land, factories and so on by individuals

cooperative business owned by people grouping together for the common good

democratic a system where decisions are made, governments elected by a free and fair voting system

depression a slump in the economy

deregulation taking away government control of what firms can and cannot do

developed world countries that have gained wealth and influence through economic strength and development of industry

developing world countries that are trying to improve their economies. They are mostly agricultural, with low incomes and therefore low savings.

discrimination favouring one group over another because of race, sex, or religion

e-commerce using the Internet for business

economist person who studies how an economy works

economy the work done, the money earned, the wages spent, the goods produced in a single country

elite group of people at the top of society

empire countries ruled by another

enclosure fences put around open land in the 16th to the 18th centuries in Britain, which drove many people from the countryside and into the cities

epidemic outbreak of disease affecting many individuals

ethnic national, racial

ethnic cleansing expelling or killing people from geographical areas or countries because they are of the 'wrong' ethnic group

exclusion prevented from engaging in normal life enjoyed by others

gene inherited element of a living thing's make-up

Gross Domestic Product (GDP) the total money spent on goods and services in a country

Gross National Product (GNP) the total money spent on goods and services, plus income earned from investments abroad

HIV/AIDS Human Immunodeficiency Virus, and its later stage, Acquired Immunodeficiency Syndrome

illiteracy inability to read or write

import product brought into a country

indigenous a person born in a particular region

infant mortality number of children dying before their first birthday per thousand live births

inflation rising prices

infrastructure the elements of an economy that make the other parts work smoothly, for example railways, roads, power stations

innate inborn, inherited

International Monetary Fund (IMF) a branch of the United Nations, founded to promote international trade and monetary cooperation, and give financial aid to states

IQ (Intelligence Quotient) measure of intelligence

malnutrition lack of the essential nutrients and food needed to maintain complete health

militia irregular fighting unit or self-defence group, often under the command of a warlord

monopolize take complete control of the production and supply of an item

Nazi follower of Adolf Hitler and the National Socialist Party in Germany

neo-Nazi modern believer in the theories of Nazism and Adolf Hitler

oral re-hydration therapy (ORT) salt and sugar solution that prevents the dehydration associated with diarrhoeal diseases and raises the chances of full recovery

peer pressure going along with the crowd

pension money paid to a retired worker. Many people are encouraged to pay part of their wages while working into a pension fund.

prejudice preconceived ideas about people's attitudes, intelligence or abilities

recession minor economic depression

refugee person forced from their home by war or natural disaster

resources supply of money, labour, raw materials and so on that can be used by a country

sanitation clean water and improved sewage disposal

shantytown squatted area that has grown up in and around a major city of the developing world

share certificate issued by a company on a stock market to raise money

socialism the equal distribution of wealth between all and the common ownership of land, factories, banks and so on

sociologist person who studies society

sterilization surgery to prevent people having children

stockbroker person who buys and sells shares

tax money collected by government from wages and profits to fund such things as education, health and pensions

underdeveloped a country that has resources – land, labour, natural resources – that are not being used

uprising rebellion against the established order or authorities

World Bank the International Bank for Reconstruction and Development, established in 1945 to raise living standards in the developing world. Affiliated to the United Nations (UN).

Contacts and helplines

THE CATHOLIC FUND FOR OVERSEAS DEVELOPMENT (CAFOD)
Romero Close, Stockwell Road,
London SW9 9TY
020 7733 7900 – www.cafod.org.uk

CHILD POVERTY ACTION GROUP
94 White Lion Street, London N1 9PF
020 7837 7979 – www.cpag.org.uk

THE CHILDREN'S SOCIETY
Public Enquiry Point
The Children's Society, Edward Rudolf House,
Margery Street, London WC1X 0JL
020 7841 4436
www.the-childrens-society.org.uk

CHRISTIAN AID
35 Lower Marsh, Waterloo,
London SE1 7RT
020 7620 4444 – www.christian-aid.org.uk

THE JOSEPH ROWNTREE FOUNDATION
The Homestead, 40 Water End, York,
North Yorkshire YO30 6WP
01904 629241 – www.jrf.org.uk

JUBILEE 2000 (DEBT CAMPAIGN)
1 Rivington Street, London EC2A 3DT
020 7739 1000 – www.jubilee2000.com
(Also visit: Netaid – www.netaid.org)

OXFAM
Oxfam House, 274 Banbury Road,
Oxford OX2 7DZ
01865 313600 – www.oxfam.org.uk

SAVE THE CHILDREN FUND (UK)
17 Grove Lane, London SE5 8RD
020 7703 5400 – www.scfuk.org.uk

SHELTER: THE NATIONAL CAMPAIGN FOR HOMELESS PEOPLE
88 Old Street, London EC1V 9HU
020 7505 4699 – www.shelter.org.uk

GOVERNMENT INFORMATION SERVICES
Social Exclusion Unit – www.cabinet-office.gov.uk/seu/
Department of the Environment, Transport and the Regions (DETR) – www.detr.gov.uk
Health Development Agency – www.hda-online.org.uk
Our Healthier Nation – www.ohn.gov.uk (Website produced by the HDA for the Department of Health)
LifeBytes: website giving young people aged 11–14 facts about health – www.lifebytes.gov.uk
Mindbodysoul: health website for young people aged 15–18 – www.mindbodysoul.gov.uk

UNITED NATIONS ORGANIZATIONS
United Nations Children's Fund (UNICEF) www.unicef.org
United Nations High Commission for Refugees (UNHCR) – www.unhcr.ch
World Health Organization (WHO) www.who.int
Joint United Nations Programme on HIV/AIDS (UNAIDS) – www.unaids.org
The World Bank – www.worldbank.org
The International Monetary Fund (IMF) – www.imf.org

Newspapers

Many quality newspapers carry computerized databases of past articles – use their search engines to find out about poverty, debt crisis, health – for example:
The Guardian – www.guardianunlimited.co.uk
The Independent – www.independent.co.uk
The Daily Telegraph – www.telegraph.co.uk
BBC – news.bbc.co.uk
ITN – www.itn.co.uk

In Australia

Australian Charities – a very useful website directory of all the major charities – www.auscharity.org
Community Aid Abroad (Oxfam)
156 George Street, Fitzroy Victoria 3065, Australia
+61 (0)3 9289 9444 – www.caa.org.au

Labornet: information about trade unions in Australia – www.labor.org.au
The Australian – national newspaper website – www.news.com.au

Government Organizations

AusAID The Australian Overseas Aid Program
GPO Box 887, Canberra ACT 2601, Australia
+61 (0)2 6206 4000 – www.ausaid.gov.au
Health and Family Services (carries a range of links to other websites) – www.health.gov.au

Aboriginal and Torres Strait Islander Commission – www.atsic.gov.au
Australian Bureau of Statistics – www.abs.gov.au
Department of Immigration and Multicultural affairs – www.immi.gov.au
Commonwealth Dept of Family & Community Services
GPO Box 7788, Canberra Mail Centre
Canberra ACT 2610
www.facs.gov.au

Further reading

Fiction and personal memoirs

The Bed and Breakfast Star
Jacqueline Wilson, Nick Sharratt (Illustrator), Yearling Books

To Kill a Mockingbird
Harper Lee, Heinemann Educational

Brave New World
Aldous Huxley, Flamingo

Of Mice and Men
John Steinbeck, Elaine Steinbeck, Mandarin

The Grapes of Wrath
John Steinbeck, Mandarin

1984
Animal Farm
Down and Out in Paris and London
The Road to Wigan Pier
George Orwell, Penguin

Eva's Story
Evelyn Julia Kent, Eva Schloss, Castle Kent

Flo: Child Migrant from Liverpool
Flo Hickson, Anne Bott (Editor), Plowright Press

Non-fiction

The American West
Colin Shephard, Dave Martin, John Murray

Britain and the Slave Trade
Rosemary Rees, Heinemann Educational

Child Labour
Sandy Hobbs et al., ABC Clio

The Great Power Conflict After 1945
Peter Fisher, Stanley Thornes

The Holocaust
Reg Grant, Hodder Wayland

Mastering Modern World History
Norman Lowe, Macmillan Press Ltd

Modern Britain, Andrew Langley et al.
Heinemann Library

Native Peoples of North America
Susan Edmonds (Ed), Cambridge University Press

Profiles: Nelson Mandela
Sean Connolly, Heinemann Library

The New Deal: America 1932–45
J. Brooman, Longman

Riding the Rails: Teenagers on the Move During the Great Depression
Errol Lincoln Uys, TV Books Inc

Russia and the USSR: Pupil's Book
Terry Fiehn, John Murray

South Africa During the Years of Apartheid
Rob Sieborger et al., John Murray

Twentieth Century History
Tony McAleavy (Ed) et al., Cambridge University Press

Index

Africa 19, 20, 21, 25, 34, 40, 41
alcohol and drug addictions 14, 23
apartheid 25, 29, 41
asylum-seekers 11
Australia 9, 11, 16, 37
The Bell Curve 28-9
Brazil 17, 24-5, 35, 40-1, 43
Britain 7, 8, 9, 11, 12-15, 22-3, 26, 27, 30-1, 37, 38-9, 43
cancer 12-13, 17
caste system 6
children
    child labour 10
    child soldiers 8, 21, 34
    education 30-1, 34
    infant and child mortality 11, 12, 17, 18, 24, 41
    poverty 9, 15, 31
cholera 12, 19
Committee to Democratize Information Technology (CDI) 35, 43
competition 5
cooperatives 43
coronary heart disease (CHD) 13, 17
credit unions 43
crime 23, 25
Cuba 41
cycle of deprivation 26, 27
debt 35, 40-1
democracy 4, 6
dependency culture 26, 28
deregulation 27
developing countries
    debt 35, 40-1
    education 10, 30, 34-5, 43
    health 10, 18, 19, 21, 43
    housing 10, 24-5
    poverty 9, 10, 42
diseases 12-13, 15, 17, 18, 19, 22

economic depression 36-7, 38, 41
economic policies 26, 38-9
education
    in developing countries 10, 34-5
    higher education 32-3
    primary and secondary education 30-1, 35
    private education 30-1
elites 6, 24, 27, 28, 29
environmental problems 43
Ethiopia 19, 40
ethnic cleansing 42
eugenics 28, 29
famines 18, 19
feudal system 6
genetics 5, 29
Germany 28, 29, 37
Great Depression 36-7, 38
Gross Domestic Product (GDP) 39
Gross National Product (GNP) 16, 17, 21, 25, 41, 43
health 10, 12-21
HIV/AIDS 19, 20-1, 25, 30
housing 10, 22-5
illiteracy 34
income inequalities 8, 9, 10, 24, 40
indigenous peoples 9, 11, 16-17
inflation 27, 39
intelligence and social standing 5, 28-9
interest rates 40
International Monetary Fund (IMF) 35, 41, 43
IQ, income and 28-9
Keynes, John Maynard 38, 43
land reform 42
life expectancy 11, 12, 24, 25, 43
malnutrition 17, 18-19, 20
market forces 26, 27
mental health 13
Mexico 17, 37
migration 10, 11, 25
monopolization of information and technology 42

mortality rates 11, 12, 16, 17, 18, 19, 20, 24, 41
natural disasters 42, 43
neo-Nazism 43
New Deal 38, 39, 43
New Zealand 8, 11, 17
Oxbridge 32-3
Pakistan 35
poverty
    causes of 40-1
    defining 9
    relative poverty 9
    subsistence level 9
racial harassment 23
refugees 10, 11, 19, 35
resources, division of 5
Right To Buy (RTB) policy 23
rural communities 23
Russia 15, 39, 43
sanitation 10, 19, 22, 25
schools 4, 30-1
self-help 43
sex trade 10, 34
shantytowns 24-5, 35
Sierra Leone 11, 34, 42
single parents 9, 14, 26
smoking 13, 14
social classes 6, 7, 32, 33
social exclusion 17, 23
social mobility 7
socialism 39
South Africa 24, 25, 29
stock market 36
strokes 13, 17
Switzerland 17
truancy 31
tuberculosis (TB) 15
Uganda 21
underclass 26-7, 42
unemployment 12, 13, 14, 15, 23, 26, 27, 37, 38, 39
United Nations Declaration of Human Rights 35
United States 11, 15, 17, 28, 29, 36-7, 39, 41, 43
universities 32-3
Wall Street Crash 36, 37
welfare state 26, 28, 43
World Bank 9, 10, 35, 40, 43

48